GW00373825

Renfrew

in old picture postcards

by
John Fyfe Anderson, B.A.

European Library - Zaltbommel/Netherlands MCMLXXXVIII

GB   ISBN 90 288 4643 3 / CIP

© 1988 European Library - Zaltbommel/Netherlands

European Library in Zaltbommel/Netherlands publishes among other things the following series:

IN OLD PICTURE POSTCARDS *is a series of books which sets out to show what a particular place looked like and what life was like in Victorian and Edwardian times. A book about virtually every town in the United Kingdom is to be published in this series. By the end of this year about 300 different volumes will have appeared. 1,500 books have already been published devoted to the Netherlands with the title* **In oude ansichten.** *In Germany, Austria and Switzerland 650, 100 and 25 books have been published as* **In alten Ansichten;** *in France by the name* **En cartes postales anciennes** *and in Belgium as* **In oude prentkaarten** *and/or* **En cartes postales anciennes** *150 respectively 400 volumes have been published.*

For further particulars about published or forthcoming books, apply to your bookseller or direct to the publisher.

INTRODUCTION

The town of Renfrew lies close to the south bank of the River Clyde. It is three miles north-east of Paisley and five miles west of Glasgow. Renfrew means 'point of the current'. This refers to the confluence of the rivers Gryffe and Clyde. The last official population figures given in 1986 showed that there were 21,300 people living in the town. Renfrew was formerly a Royal Burgh with its own provost, bailies and town councillors. However, with the reorganisation of local government in 1975 it ceased to have these privileges and became part of the newly formed Renfrew District Council.

The Burgh of Renfrew was founded circa 1124 by King David I. The parish of Renfrew is distinguished because of its connection with the ancient house of Stewart, the lands of Renfrew were the first mentioned in the estates specified in the charter granted by King Malcolm IV in 1157 in favour of Walter Fitz Alan, the first High Steward of Scotland.

Walter, the sixth High Steward of Scotland, married Princess Marjory Bruce, daughter of King Robert the Bruce, in 1315. Their son, King Robert II, became the first monarch in the Stewart line. The present British Royal Family is descended from the Stewarts. H.R.H. the Prince of Wales is the Great Steward of Scotland. He is also the Baron of Renfrew, which was a title originally granted to the heir to the Scottish throne by the Burgh of Renfrew in 1404.

Renfrew was made a Royal Burgh in 1396 after having received a charter from King Robert III. This bestowed certain rights concerning foreign trade and also permitted annual fairs to be held. Subsequent confirmatory charters were granted by King James VI in 1575 and also in 1614 when that monarch had become King James I of the United Kingdoms of Scotland and England. In 1614 the burgh was the principal port on the Clyde.

By 1836 the parish minister, the Reverend Duncan Macfarlan, was writing that the manufactures in the parish were various though not extensive. He listed among them muslin weaving, a bleachfield, a tile work and a distillery.

It was in the 1840s that shipbuilding first became prominent in Renfrew. The first shipbuilding firm was Barr and McNab which was established in 1844. This firm was later acquired by James Henderson and Son, who commenced business in 1847. Further reorganisation of the firm took place in 1895 under the name of Lobnitz and Company. The famous shipbuilding firm of William Simons and Company moved to Renfrew in 1860.

The establishment of Babcock and Wilcox Ltd. in 1895 was important for the growth of Renfrew. From the time Babcock's came to Renfrew, the population increase was considerable. In 1891 the population of the town was 6,764, while by 1911 this figure had increased to 12,565. However, after 1911 the population grew more slowly. During the 1930s there was much unemployment and many people moved to England for work or emigrated overseas.

Carntyne Steel Castings moved to Renfrew from Glasgow in 1907 and the Clyde Rubber Company was established in the town in 1912. Further employment was created in 1938 with the building of Hillington Industrial Estate which was within the burgh boundary. This was the first industrial estate of its type to be situated in Scotland. In the same year the firm of Scottish Cables Ltd. was founded in Renfrew by William Fraser.

During the First World War, 1914-1918, the shipyards were extremely busy as a result of building ships for the Royal Navy. Babcock and Wilcox also manufactured marine boilers for the Navy. A large factory was also built at Babcock's for the production of shells for the armed forces.

A certain amount of damage took place in Renfrew during the Second World War, 1939-1945. The wharf near the Ferry was destroyed at the time of the Clydebank Blitz on 13th March 1941. During the war incendiary bombs were dropped on many parts of the burgh. Sandbags were laid along each street in order to prevent further damage from the air raids.

Renfrew has gone through many changes in its long history. There is no trace left of Renfrew Castle, once the main residence of the Stewards of Scotland. The old houses at Renfrew Cross possessed great character and their demolition at the beginning of this century was a great loss. This is also true regarding the great houses of Elderslie and Blythswood, which have met a similar fate.

However, some fine buildings still remain, such as the Town Hall and Renfrew Parish Church. The great benefactions of the Robertson Park and the Victory Baths still give much pleasure to the people of the town.

The author hopes that the following illustrations will be of interest to the people of Renfrew, and also to those who have had an association with the town in the past.

Acknowledgements:

The author wishes to acknowledge the assistance of the following individuals in the preparation of this book: Mr. and Mrs. Tomlinson, Ness Castle, Inverness; Mrs. Patricia M. Rodger, Selby, North Yorkshire; Mrs. M. Youell, Radford, Coventry; Mrs. Margaret K. Muirhead, Livingston, West Lothian; Mrs. Margaret Pedder, Port Bannatyne, Bute; Mrs. M. Cram, Barrow-in-Furness, Cumbria; and Mr. John Moir of Renfrew Historical Society. Thanks are also due to the Local History Department, Renfrew District Libraries; Renfrew Community Library; Strathclyde Regional Archives, Mitchell Library, Glasgow for illustrations 4, 5, 6, 7, 8 and 10; and St. Andrews University Library for permission to reproduce the pictures of Blythswood House and Renfrew Pipe Band.

Bibliography:

J. Cowan, *From Glasgow's Treasure Chest,* Glasgow 1951.

K. Davies, *The Clyde Passenger Steamers,* Ayr, 1980.

J.A. Dunn, *History of Renfrew.*

F.H. Groome, *Ordnance Gazeteer of Scotland,* volume 6, 1885.

The Old Country Houses of the Old Glasgow Gentry, 2nd edition, Glasgow, 1878.

Rev. D.M. Swanson, *The Parish and Burgh of Renfrew,* Third Statistical Account, 1962.

F.A. Walker, *The South Clyde Estuary,* Edinburgh, 1986.

J. Walls and G. Hamilton, *The Renfrew Ferry,* Renfrew, 1984.

Paisley and Renfrewshire Gazette, 1880-1930.

1. *Queen Victoria's visit.* **Her Majesty Queen Victoria visited Renfrew on 22nd August 1888. In this photograph she is the figure seated in the open carriage nearest the specially erected platform in Hairst Street, where Her Majesty was officially received by Provost Daniel Wright. Opposite the platform and in front of the Town Hall a company of one hundred men from the different companies of the 2nd Volunteer Battalion, Princess Louise Argyll and Sutherland Highlanders were drawn up as a guard of honour under the command of Hon. Major Wood. The town was extensively decorated for the Queen's visit, especially the Town Hall which was surrounded by a draping of blue cloth with trophies of flags and shields in addition. Over the main entrance of the Town Hall there was the coat of arms of H.R.H. the Prince of Wales with the crown in the centre. The Royal Standard flew from the top of the tower and was visible for miles around. Before the departure of the Queen for Glasgow, over a thousand children sang the National Anthem from a stand which had been erected in Fulbar Street.**

2. *Royal Arch.* On her visit to Renfrew, Queen Victoria was the guest of Sir Archibald Campbell, later Lord Blythswood, at Blythswood House. This triumphal arch was erected at the entrance to the Blythswood Estate in Inchinnan Road. The arch was made of evergreens in the form of a baronial gateway, surmounted by a crown and various international flags. It was the work of the head gardener Mr. Methven and his assistants. The Queen was driven in an open carriage to Blythswood House soon after her arrival by the Royal Train at the private platform, which had been erected as a continuation of the west side of Fulbar Street Station. It is recorded that on this occasion Her Majesty wore a plain black dress. This Royal Visit was a momentous occasion for Renfrew. New official robes were provided for the Provost and Magistrates, and the 22nd August 1888 was observed as a general holiday in honour of the Queen's visit. There were special regulations for traffic during the visit and fireworks displays were held on the evenings of 22nd and 23rd August.

BLYTHSWOOD HOUSE, RENFREW.

3. *Blythswood House 1904.* Blythswood House was situated on the right bank of the Black Cart, near its junction with the Clyde. This magnificent edifice was built during 1820-1822 for Major Archibald Campbell who at that time was the Member of Parliament for the Glasgow District of Burghs which included Glasgow, Rutherglen, Renfrew and Dumbarton. The name of the estate on which the mansion was built was Ranfield. It was purchased in 1654 by Provost Colin Campbell of Glasgow from Mr. John Hay of Renfrew. There was an ancient mansion on Ranfield which continued to be the residence of the Campbells of Blythswood till 1821. The architect of the new mansion was Mr. Gillespie Graham who designed it according to the Greek Revival Style. Many members of the Royal Family resided at Blythswood House when they were visiting Glasgow or Renfrew. Indeed, there can be few mansions in Scotland which have had such an impressive record of Royal visits. Another famous visitor was the poet and novelist Sir Walter Scott, who came to Blythswood in 1827 to see his kinsman, Archibald Campbell. Blythswood House was demolished in 1935. The fairways of Renfrew Golf Club now run through the former site of this great mansion.

4. *Library*. This photograph shows the magnificent library at Blythswood House. The collection of books was assembled by Archibald Campbell, the father of the first Lord Blythswood. The range of books included works on ornithology, architecture, travel, entomology, and archaeology. One of the most important books in this collection was a copy of the poems of Robert Burns which had been owned by the poet. On the fly leaf of this book Burns had written 'The Farewell', which was composed in 1786 when he was thinking of travelling to the West Indies. All of the furniture in the library is of the finest quality. A row of busts can also be seen on top of the bookcases.

5. *Drawing room.* This is the richly furnished drawing room of Blythswood House. All of the fittings are of the best quality and there is much attention to detail. Two beautiful vases adorn the mantelpiece beside the clock which is under a glass dome. A high standard of workmanship can be seen in the design of the fireplace. The drawing room also contained a fine painted ceiling which was executed by Italian artists in 1850. The other reception rooms were much admired for their fine proportions and contained paintings by famous artists.

6. *Sculpture gallery*. The gallery extended the entire length of the mansion-house of Blythswood. The sculptures shown here were some of the many objects which were sold by auction in March 1930 along with all of the furniture and effects of Blythswood House. The auctioneers were Messrs. Morrison, McChlery and Co. of Glasgow. There was much interest shown in this sale and dealers came from all over the country to purchase such items as Louis XV reproduction furniture, china, candelabra, bronzes, old weapons and books. Two ancient swords, which were over 2,000 years old, were purchased by the eighth Duke of Atholl.

7. *Morning room.* There are numerous objects in this photograph of the morning room of Blythswood House. Candelabra hang from the ceiling, there is a guitar lying on the chair near the door and there are pictures on the walls. The most striking feature is the large Masonic symbol on the wall above the mantelpiece. This is surrounded by smaller Masonic symbols. The first Lord Blythswood was at one time Grand Master Mason of Scotland.

8. *Sir Archibald Campbell (first Lord Blythswood).* When this photograph was taken in the 1880s, Sir Archibald had not yet been raised to the peerage. Here he is master of all he surveys as he poses with two ghillies and dogs beside the massive pillars of Blythswood House. The ghillie on the right of the picture is wearing a kilt. These ghillies were servants who would attend Sir Archibald when he was engaged in a field sports such as shooting.

9. *Lord Blythswood.* The figure on the left of this photograph is Archibald Campbell, first Lord Blythswood, who is seen here at a curling match on his estate in the 1890s. He was born in 1837 and died in 1908. In 1864 he married the Hon. Augusta Clementina Carrington, daughter of the second Lord Carrington. Archibald Campbell was for a time Captain and Lieutenant Colonel of the Scots Guards with whom he served in the Crimean War of 1854-1856, when he was severely wounded. He succeeded to the Blythswood Estate in 1868 and was Member of Parliament for the Western Division of Renfrewshire from 1873 to 1874, and also from 1885 to 1892. His other positions included being Vice-Lieutenant and Convener of the County of Renfrew and Colonel of the 4th Battalion Princess Louise Argyll and Sutherland Highlanders. In addition he was Colonel and A.D.C. to H.M. Queen Victoria. Colonel Campbell was created a baronet in 1880 and raised to the peerage in 1892. He was also an enthusiastic amateur scientist and carried out experiments on X-rays.

10. *Family group*. Members of the Campbell family pose for the camera on the portico of Blythswood House in the 1880s. Three of the younger members of the family and wearing the kilt. Everyone looks rather glum in this photograph. It was obviously not the custom to smile at the camera in these days!

11. *Curling match.* This photograph shows the other participants in the curling match. Lord Blythswood, wearing a cape, can be seen standing fourth from the right. There is quite a variety of headgear to be seen here. Four of the gentlemen, including Lord Blythswood, have luxuriant beards.

12. *First Steam Ferry (1).* This is a photograph of the first steam powered ferry which was built by T. Wingate and Company of Whiteinch. This ferry was in service from 1868 to 1897, conveying passengers and goods from Renfrew to Yoker on the opposite bank of the River Clyde. It was operated by means of a single chain which passed over a steam driven cog. This chain which was firmly secured on both river banks was very heavy and lay on the river-bed. Thus, vessels which were sailing up and down the river did not become entangled with the ferry chain. A large hand-operated wheel which extended above the deck was used to raise and lower the landing platforms. On the whole, this method worked satisfactorily. However, problems did occur at low tides when it was difficult to make a good landing.

13. *First Steam Ferry (2).* Here the ferry is seen on the Renfrew side with the Ferry Inn in the background. The chimney of the Gasworks in Ferry Road can be seen to the left of the crane. The tower of the Town Hall can just be discerned above the trees on the left. This photograph was taken about 1892.

Renfrew Ferry

14. *Second Steam Ferry.* Passengers are seen here on the Renfrew ferry in 1905. The first steam driven ferry had been introduced in 1868. The second steam ferry, shown here, commenced operations at Renfrew in 1897, and was in service until 1912. This was larger and faster than the first ferry as it had double chains. The accommodation for vehicles had also been improved as four carts could now be carried, while the previous ferry could hardly carry four. The second steam ferry was made of steel and built by S. McKnight and Company of Ayr. A third steam ferry came into service in 1912 and was in use until 1935. These ferries transported goods and passengers across the River Clyde from Renfrew to Yoker on the opposite bank.

15. *Renfrew Ferry*. This is the second steam ferry at Renfrew in the form of a greetings card. The attractive coat of arms of the Burgh of Renfrew is also shown here. It was granted to Renfrew by the Lord Lyon King of Arms from the Lyon Court in Edinburgh in July 1676. The burgh arms consist of a vessel with the sun over the prow and the moon over the stern, with two crosses, one fore and another aft. At the top of the mast of the ship is a flag with a St. Andrew's cross, and from the yard-arm hang two shields, one bearing a lion rampant, which is the Royal coat of arms for Scotland, and the other with the arms of the Stewarts. The motto is 'Deus gubernat navem' which means 'God is the pilot of the ship'. The significance of Renfrew as a port is emphasised by this coat of arms.

RELIABLE SERIES 687.

At the Ferry, Renfrew

16. *At the Ferry*. A magnificent sailing ship dominates the river in this view of 1907. Passengers are seen here on the second steam ferry. The rails shown on the right are for the trams, and it is likely that these passengers would have travelled to the ferry by tram.

Ferry Green, Renfrew

17. *Ferry Green*. Two smartly dressed little girls pose for the camera beside the base of the enormous flag-pole on Ferry Green in about 1912. There are also two men who are sitting by the river bank and looking intently at the photographer. The ferry can be seen on the opposite bank of the Clyde. A fine example of a wrought iron fountain is also shown here, but it is no longer to be found on this site.

Looking from the Ferry. Renfrew.

18. *Looking from the Ferry*. This view dates from about 1900. The building on the left is the Ferry Inn which was built in 1829. It was one of the first buildings to have gas lighting when this was introduced to Renfrew in the 1840s. A gas lamp can be seen attached to the wall of the inn. Beneath it a family is waiting for the ferry to take them across to Yoker. The boy is wheeling a barrow which contains the luggage. The lady in the foreground is dressed in the fashion of the time with a very large hat, long coat and dress.

19. *Ferry Road.* This is a view of Ferry Road in the 1890s. The road surface is not in good condition and the marks of the horse-drawn carts can be seen clearly. Part of the Gasworks can be seen on the left of the terraced houses. These houses have been demolished. This road led down to the ferry. The end of an era came in June 1984 when the last chain driven Renfrew ferry made its final crossing of the Clyde.

THE CLYDE AT RENFREW FERRY, RENFREW.

20. *The Clyde at Renfrew Ferry.* The paddle steamer 'Isle of Arran' is sailing past Renfrew Ferry in this scene from about 1910. At this time many paddle steamers were to be seen on the Clyde which is no longer the case to-day. The 'Isle of Arran' was built by T. Seath of Rutherglen in 1892. During the First World War of 1914-1918, she was converted to a minesweeper, but returned to normal service at the end of the war. The 'Isle of Arran' was in service on the Clyde until 1933. In that year she was told to the General Steam Navigation Company Ltd. for service on the Thames. In 1936 this paddle steamer was sold for scrapping.

21. *Castlehill House*. This photograph was taken in the 1890s. Castlehill House occupied a site a short distance back from Ferry Road. The building on the right of the picture is the gable-end of the Free Church in Renfield Street. About 1836 there was a smaller house on this site. The family who lived there at that time were called Bryce. They were succeeded in residence by Mr. William Simons, the founder of the firm of dredger builders which bears his name. The next owner was Mr. Andrew Brown, the shipbuilder and former Provost of Renfrew. In the mid-1880s he rebuilt the house and added greatly to its size. Castlehill House was continuously occupied until 1933, but lay empty till 1936 when it was demolished.

22. *Inchinnan Road*. This shows Inchinnan Road in the mid-1890s looking from St. Andrew's Cross. The block of tenements on the right extends into Hairst Street. To the left of the tenements are the sites which were later occupied by the Victory Baths and the Police Station. The tenements are still standing, but the draper's shop is now a take-away restaurant and tea-room.

23. *South End of Queen Street.* Two small boys sit on the kerb of a traffic-free Queen Street at the end of the last century. The low-roofed building on the left was formerly dairy premises occupied by Mr. Adam Stewart. The house on the right has been demolished. However, the two-storeyed house between these two buildings still remains in position.

24. *Renfrew Wharf.* This view looks towards Renfrew Ferry in the closing years of last century. The house in the distance is in Yoker on the opposite bank of the Clyde. The third building from the left is the Ferry Inn. Ferdy Coia's café was formerly located in the second building from the left. William Simons and Company used the crane for the fitting out of dredgers in the Pudzeoch.

25. *Dye Works.* Mr. John Bell's Dye Works were situated at the east end of Renfrew where Glebe Street now joins High Street. The Dye Works were formerly Clark's Bleach Works. The site on the right of this picture is now occupied by the Research Centre of Babcock Power Ltd. This photograph was taken in about 1890.

24509   **CANAL STREET, RENFREW**   **VALENTINES SERIES**

26. *Canal Street about 1899.* A horse and cart can be seen in this street scene. Two other horses and carts can be faintly discerned on the left of this postcard. A man on the right is carrying something on his head, which seems rather unusual. The houses on the left were demolished in order to make way for the new tenements which were built in Canal Street at the beginning of this century.

27. *Old Gasworks, 1900.* The Pudzeoch is in the foreground here. The houses are in Ferry Road. Gasworks at Renfrew were first built in 1840. In 1892 the increased demands on the supply necessitated the construction of a new retort house, exhauster and set of purifiers. In that year the quantity of gas manufactured was 13 million cubic feet. However, the new extension was capable of dealing with an annual output of 26 million cubic feet. Extensive additions to the Gasworks were formally opened in 1908. By this time the annual output of gas amounted to 47 million cubic feet.

28. *Queen Street.* This is a view of Queen Street in about 1900. In the 1870s Garlick's Smithy was to be found in Queen Street. During the Second World War of 1939-1945 there was considerable bomb damage in the street due to German air raids. The Masonic Hall was bombed twice and two cottages were demolished by bombs. Today the appearance of Queen Street is completely different from the view which is shown here.

29. *Wilson Street.* This is a photograph of Wilson Street towards the end of last century. A boot repairer's shop can be seen on the left of the picture. There is a butcher's shop on the right where the carcase of a sheep can be seen hanging. An apprentice butcher wearing his long apron is standing in the street. Two small girls are seen wearing the smocks which were the fashion of the time. The old low roofed cottages seem strangely out of place with the other buildings.

30. *Manse Street.* This is a photograph of Manse Street which was taken in the late 1890s. Two small boys can be seen outside the old cottage which formerly stood at Renfrew Cross. There is a prominent sign in the street which advertises the plumbing and gasfitting business of James Whyte and Son. The appearance of Manse Street today is completely different from this photograph as all the houses which are shown here have been demolished.

31. *Group in High Street.* This is a photograph of a rather serious looking group of Renfrew people in the 1890s. Most of them would be quite unaccustomed to being photographed. The thatched roofs of the cottages and the cobble-stone street are of special interest here. The faint outline of the Town Hall can just be seen in the distance.

32. *High Street.* This shows a group of children in High Street in the 1900s. Some of them are barefooted, but most of the boys are wearing caps. It seems amazing in the present day that such a photograph could be taken as there is now constant traffic in this street. This was obviously not the case here, and even the probable approach of a tram does not seem to worry these children. The narrowness of High Street is evident here. The Parish Church Manse was located in this street in the 1870s. At the same period Bell's Dye Works was situated at the far end of the same street.

33. *Renfrew Parish Church.* This is an early photograph of Renfrew Parish Church which was then in a much more rural setting than it is now. The church which is located to the south of High Street was erected in 1861-1862. The architect was J.T. Rochead who designed it according to the style known as lancet Gothic. The 130 ft. spire is of exceptional quality and is one of the finest in Scotland. Inside the church is the Ross Vault which contains nine wooden caskets with inner leaden coffins three of which contain members of the Ross family and six have the remains of members of the family of the Earl of Glasgow. The earliest dated coffin is that of James, sixth Lord Ross who died in 1633. Alterations to the chancel were made in 1908 by P. MacGregor Chalmers. The Reverend Robert Stephen, M.A. was minister of the church for 39 years from 1858 to 1897. His successor was the Reverend George Anderson, D.D. who served as minister from 1898 to 1916. He was succeeded by the Reverend David Young who was parish minister from 1916 to 1933.

34. *Renfrew Free Church*. This is a photograph of Renfrew Free Church in Renfield Street which was taken in about 1900. The manse can be seen on the right. The church was built on the same site as the previous Free Church. Renfrew Free Church was one of the first of the Free Churches to be erected in Scotland after the Disruption of 1843 when almost one third of the ministers in Scotland seceded from the Church of Scotland. The church of 1883, shown here, is in the Plain Gothic Style and has a squat square tower with pinnacles. The first minister was the Reverend Dr. Duncan Macfarlan who served from 1843 to 1853. He was succeeded by the Reverend David Neilson who was minister from 1853 to 1890. His successor was the Reverend Dr. Robert Hill who served as minister at this church from 1891 to 1931. This church later became the North United Free Church. It is now the North Parish Church of Scotland.

RENFIELD ST.

35. *Renfield Street (1).* This shows the Free Church in Renfield Street about 1910. It provides an interesting contrast to the previous picture. The cottage on the left of the church has been demolished and tenements have been erected. As a result, the church has lost its position of dominance in the street. The elderly woman here seems to be quite happy as she walks down the middle of the street on her way to the shops. A number of boys are also to be seen in the background and there is a small child who is crouched on the pavement at the base of the lamp-post on the right of the picture.

36. *Renfield Street (2).* This is a view of Renfield Street looking towards Canal Street in about 1909. The cottage on the right, which looks somewhat out of place beside the tenements, was later demolished. The site is now occupied by the premises of the Royal Bank of Scotland who have a branch in Canal Street. The building on the left has also been demolished to be replaced by a block of tenements which include shops. This block also includes Renfrew Post Office in Canal Street. Renfield Street was named after the former Ranfield Estate which later became the Blythswood Estate. A slightly different mode of spelling was adopted for the street with 'Ranfield' changing to 'Renfield'.

37. *Renfrew Cross.* This is Renfrew Cross in 1900. All of the buildings on the left of the picture have been demolished. The premises of Mr. John Cumming's butcher's shop can be seen to the right of the fountain. The word 'flesher' is written on the sign above the shop. This is the old Scots word for a butcher which is less commonly used today. A wooden step-ladder can be seen propped against the wall of Mr. Leslie Kirk's painting and decorating business. There is a doctor's surgery and dispensary to be found in the building on the left of the fountain. The Town Hall is immediately to the right of the four lamp-posts. It was at this location opposite the Town Hall that Queen Victoria was officially welcomed on her visit to Renfrew in 1888.

38. *Houses at Renfrew Cross.* A clerical gentleman engages in conversation outside the tobacconist's shop at Renfrew Cross at the beginning of the century. The thatched house with the outside stairs leading to the upper storey is an interesting feature here. The houses on the left of the picture are in Manse Street. Unfortunately none of these buildings remain standing and, as a result, much of the character of the old Renfrew Cross has been lost.

39. *View from Town Hall Steeple.* This photograph shows the old-world charm of the area near Renfrew Cross in the last century. The street on the left is Canal Street with Manse Street on the right. The building with the three flag-poles is the business premises of Robert Lang who was a spirit merchant.

40. *View of Canal Street*. This shows a deserted Canal Street at the beginning of the century. The low-roofed building on the right with the crow-stepped gable is the public-house, known as 'The Auld House'. Advertisements for various drinks are exhibited on the large sign which extends across the gable-end of the pub. The building which is situated at the base of the tower of the Town Hall is the Wheatsheaf Inn which was built about 1830. This is a fine photograph of the tower which occupies a commanding position over the smaller buildings in this street.

41. *Canal Street 1910*. Canal Street was originally called Ferry Road. However, after the Renfrew Canal was opened in 1786, the name was changed. The name-change particularly applied to the section of Ferry Road from the Cross to the canal. The four-storeyed tenements shown on the left of this view were built in 1900-1901. The pudding basin dome at number 48 Canal Street on the extreme left of this picture is an interesting architectural feature. The building on the right, with the two lamp-posts outside, is the Brown Institute. This was presented to the town by Andrew Brown who was Provost of Renfrew from 1867 to 1870, 1879 to 1882 and 1891 to 1900. The facilities available at the Institute consisted of a reading room, billiard room and library. Renfrew Castle once stood on the site of the Brown Institute. It was built circa 1150 by Walter FitzAlan, the first High Steward of Scotland.

42. *High Moorpark.* Children are to be seen standing all over Paisley Road in this view from the beginning of the century. It is possible that the group of children on the right were going on an outing on the approaching tramcar. The buildings here are designed in a variety of architectural styles with levels of two, three and four storeys. There is also a small cottage to be seen at the end of the four-storeyed tenements. All of these houses to the left of the tenements have been demolished.

TESTIMONIAL SCHOOL,
RENFREW

43. *Blythswood Testimonial School, 1903.* The building on the left of this postcard is the Blythswood Testimonial School which was built during 1840-1842. The architect was John Stephen, who designed it according to the Greek Revival Style. The school was built as a memorial to Archibald Campbell of Blythswood who had recently died. The necessary finance was raised by the gentlemen of the county of Renfrew. Pupils were transferred to this school in 1843 from the old Burgh School in High Street. Blythswood Testimonial became the burgh grammar school and was handed over to the town council on condition that they maintained it as a school and contributed £100 a year to its support. An extension to the school was built in 1886 and this can be seen on the right of the picture. The first headmaster was Peter McLaren, L.L.D., who served from 1843 to 1876. Successive headmasters until the 1930s were as follows: John McGlashan, F.E.I.S. (1876-1907); George Irvine, M.A. (1907-1908); William Kerr, M.A. (1908-1919); William Deans, M.A. (1920-1927); and Alex. Macdonald (1927-1938). This school has been demolished. However, a small section of the original building still remains.

Moorpark School, Renfrew.

44. *Moorpark School.* A small child peers through the iron railings which surround Moorpark Public School in 1903. The entrance for girls is on the right between the two gateposts. There was a similar entrance for the boys on the left side of the building. The headmaster at this time was Archibald Walker. He had been appointed to the position in 1897 and served till 1919. His successor was William Kerr, M.A. who served from 1919 to 1923. The next headmaster was Louis Neil Gow, M.A. who occupied the position from 1923 to 1928. In 1928 Charles Rice, M.A. was appointed headmaster and served till 1941.

45. *Glebe High School, 1913.* The official name of this school was the Renfrew High Public School. However, it was known locally as the Glebe School. It was formally opened on 11th August 1908 by the shipowner William Robertson, who had been a pupil at Blythswood Testimonial School. There were a total of 321 pupils at the school in 1908. These pupils had been transferred from Blythswood Testimonial School and included those from both primary and secondary levels. In 1919 as a result of new legislation, the school was brought under the administration of the County of Renfrew Education Authority. Prior to this time, it had been administered by the School Board of Renfrew. The school was officially designated as Renfrew High School in 1927. The site of the school was adjacent to the Renfrew Parish Church Halls. The spire of the Parish Church can be seen on the right of this view. A new Renfrew High School was opened on 18th February 1965. The first headmaster of the school was George Irving, M.A. who held this position from 1908 to 1921. He was succeeded by John W. Gibson, M.A. who served as headmaster from 1923 to 1947.

46. *Bank buildings, Renfrew Cross, 1904.* The absence of traffic is noticeable here with the group of men posing for the camera while standing in Hairst Street. The ornate lamp-posts on the left are positioned outside the Town Hall. The fountain on the opposite side of the street is another interesting feature. The turretted building at the corner of High Street and Canal Street was designed for the Bank of Scotland. The bank branch entrance can be seen underneath the turret. The architect of the building was Sir George Washington Browne. The material used in the construction was red sandstone ashlar. Attention to architectural detail is in evidence here with the decorative stonework. The window of the bank is of a particularly interesting design. The buildings in High Street on the extreme right of this view are no longer standing and the fountain has also disappeared from its position. It is now to be found near the entrance of Robertson Park in Inchinnan Road. The fountain was presented to the Burgh of Renfrew by A.C. Bryce in memory of Andrew Crawford, who was Provost of Renfrew from 1846 to 1849.

47. *Hairst Street and Town Hall.* The tower of the Town Hall dominates the skyline in this view of the 1900s. The only form of transport to be seen here is the bicycle on the right which is being wheeled by a girl. Some of the boys are in bare feet on this hot summer's day long ago. Three of them are clustered round the fountain which also acts as a signpost. The sign on the left is for Greenock and the one on the right is for Paisley. 'Hairst' in Scots means 'harvest'. Thus, Hairst Street was originally the 'harvest street' where the produce of local farms was sold. Weekly markets and fairs were also held in Hairst Street. All of the buildings on the right side of Hairst Street are no longer standing.

St. Andrew's Cross, Renfrew

48. *St. Andrew's Cross (1)*. This is a view of St. Andrew's Cross at the beginning of this century. The two horse-drawn carts in the foreground, with another to be seen in the left distance, are the only evidence of transport here. No rails for the trams had been laid at this time. The Renfrew War Memorial was later erected on a site immediately to the right of the man who is leading the horse and cart. The substantially built four-storeyed tenements with the shops underneath are in Inchinnan Road.

ST. ANDREW'S CROSS, RENFREW

49. *St. Andrew's Cross (2).* This view of 1912 shows a close-up of the tenements in Inchinnan Road on the right and Paisley on the left. The shop on the corner is appropriately named 'Blythswood House'. Next to this is a bootmaker and repairer's shop. The third shop from the left is R. Montgomerie's bakery business. The Cross was named after Saint Andrew who has been regarded as the patron saint of Scotland since about the year 750.

50. *Broadloan, Moorpark*. A varied group pose for the camera in Broadloan in 1909. The children are all very smartly dressed with the boys in their smart suits and Eton collars. The small girl on the right is wearing a wide-brimmed hat which was the fashion at this time. The horse and cart was the normal method of transporting goods at this time. The houses shown here are of high quality. Wrought iron fences can be seen on both sides of the street.

51. *Murray's Shop.* This shows Murray's shop at the corner of Bell Street and Inchinnan Road in the early years of the century. The style of dress of the workmen and children is an interesting feature here. The window displays are extremely well laid out with all types of goods. There is also an advertisement for 'Fry's Chocolate' in the window on the left. 'Mitchell's Gold Medal Golden Dawn Cigarettes' are advertised in the window on the right. The ivy-covered walls in Inchinnan Road are also of interest here. This shop would have supplied all kinds of merchandise to the people living nearby. It still functions today, but the name has been changed to 'Susan's Corner'.

Swing Bridge, Renfrew.

MUIR, STATIONER, RENFREW. R1996

52. *Swing Bridge.* This is the old wooden swing bridge over the White Cart estuary in the 1900s. It was originally erected in 1787 at a cost of £1,900. This bridge was demolished in 1919 when a temporary structure took its place until a new swing bridge was erected in 1923 by Sir William Arrol and Company at a cost of £62,500. The bridge-master's house can be seen on the right of this picture.

53. *Town Hall, Rear View.* This is a photograph of the Town Hall from Fulbar Street at the beginning of the century. The spire of Renfrew Parish Church can be seen on the right. It was in this street that Mr. Thomas Paton began his business career with a cycle repair shop. In 1921 he began a transport business with one bus. This later became the Paton Bus Company.

Paisley Road, Renfrew

Valentines Series

54. *Paisley Road*. This is a view of Paisley Road in about 1900. The semi-detached villa on the right is known as Beechcroft. This was the home of Dr. William Goldie Stevens who was Medical Officer of Health for Renfrew from 1884 to 1928. When Dr. Stevens was a medical student he studied under Lord Lister, the famous pioneer of antiseptic surgery. It was through Dr. Stevens' patient and persistent advocacy of a pure milk supply, a nutritious diet and the proper feeding of infants that the health of the Renfrew people improved. Dr. Stevens also served as a councillor and magistrate. He died in 1935 aged 94. The building on the right with the spire is Trinity Church. The foundation stone of this church was laid in August 1864 by Sir Peter Coats of Woodside, Paisley. The building of the church was completed in June 1865. Professor William Barclay, C.B.E., D.D., the well-known theologian, was minister of Trinity Church from 1933 to 1947. From 1963 to 1974 he was Professor of Divinity and Biblical Criticism at the University of Glasgow.

55. *Fulbar Street from the Station*. The steeple of the Town Hall is in the distance. The building on the left is Fulbar Street Railway Station. A railway between Renfrew and Paisley was opened in 1837. Trains ceased to run from Fulbar Street Station in September 1966.

56. *Alexandra Drive, 1905.* The house on the right is known as Monkdyke. It was once owned by Colonel Walter Brown of William Simons and Company. He also owned the ground on the left. This is now a small park. Colonel Brown left Monkdyke to the Burgh of Renfrew in his will for such use as it might decide. The house was damaged as a result of air raids in 1941. It was later restored and was used by the town clerk and his staff. There was also a council chamber, Monkdyke is now the Legal Services office of Renfrew District Council. The houses on the left of this picture are in Glebe Road.

The Pudzeoch from Bridge, Renfrew

Valentines Series

57. *The Pudzeoch.* This is a most tranquil scene, dating from about 1905. It must have been a sunny day when this scene was photographed as the trees are clearly reflected in the water. The Pudzeoch was the popular name of the Renfrew Canal which was opened in 1786. Negotiations regarding its construction had begun in 1772 between Mr. James Campbell, who was then Provost of Renfrew, and Mr. Alexander Speirs of Elderslie.

58. *Moorpark Terrace, 1906.* This is now Paisley Road. A group of children stand in the street beside the tram stop. There is a grocer's shop on the corner of Porterfield Road and the former Moorpark Terrace. These premises are now occupied by Macdonald's the chemist. The solitary lamp-post shown here would now be a collector's item.

BLYTHSWOOD ROAD, RENFREW

59. *Blythswood Road.* A man leads a horse and cart along the cobble-stone Blythswood Road in the early years of this century. This road led to the tradesmen's entrance at Blythswood House. The terraced houses here are designed to a high standard. However, there was not much lighting in this road with only two lamp-posts. One can be seen on the right while the other is at the end of the row of houses.

MUIRPARK AVENUE, MOORPARK, RENFREW.

60. *Muirpark Avenue*. Ten boys stand in Muirpark Avenue, Moorpark, in about 1909. They are all dressed in their best clothes and seven of them are wearing caps. The two-storeyed terrace houses are all of a uniform design. The wooden fence which extends along Muirpark Avenue is an interesting feature here. In the 1870s Moorpark consisted of two little clachans of houses. One was called High Moorpark and the other was called Low Moorpark.

61. *Visit of the Prince and Princess of Wales.* The Prince and Princess of Wales (later King George V and Queen Mary) visited Renfrew in April 1907. This is one of the tramcars which was specially decorated for the occasion. The Royal visitors were the guests of Lord Blythswood at Blythswood House where Queen Victoria had resided on the occasion of her visit to Renfrew in 1888. Provost Peter Ferguson had the honour of lunching with Their Royal Highnesses at Blythswood House. Very strong barricades were erected in Hairst Street for this Royal visit, and it was from behind these that the people of Renfrew welcomed the Prince and Princess on a very wet day. It was a special honour for Renfrew that the Prince of Wales should visit the town as being the heir to the throne, among his numerous titles, he was also the Baron of Renfrew.

62. *Town Hall and Steeple, 1910.* The Town Hall at Renfrew Cross replaced the old Town Hall which was built in 1670 and remained on the west side of the Cross till 1871 when it was demolished. The new building was erected during 1871-1873 at a cost of £7,500. However, this structure was partially destroyed by fire on 6th March 1878, but was soon renovated. The architect of the new Town Hall was James Lamb. After the fire of 1878, renovation work was supervised by Loudon McQueen who was clerk of works on the Blythswood Estate. The style is mixed French Gothic and at the east end of the building there is a massive square tower which rises to a height of 105 feet with corbelled turrets and ornamented cresting. This tower still occupies a commanding position in the town. The new Town Hall provided improved facilities with a public hall which had accommodation for 800 persons, a council chamber, police office and cells.

63. *Police Station.* The new Police Station in Inchinnan Road was erected at the cost of £6,000 and was opened on 13th March 1910. Prior to this time, the police occupied premises in the Town Chambers. The opening ceremony took place in the presence of members of the Town Council, public officials and the Chief Constables of Govan, Partick, Johnstone and Greenock. Mr. A.R. Paterson, the Master of Works and architect of the new building, presented Provost Robert Anderson with a golden key in the name of the contractors. The Provost thanked those who had presented him with the key and said that they would have pleasure in knowing that it would be handed down to his family as a memento. He also said that it was the key of one of the finest buildings in the neighbourhood which reflected great credit on the architect and the contractors for such fine workmanship. The new Police Station provided the much needed facilities for Captain William Robb and his men. Captain Robb was Chief Constable of Renfrew from 1909 to 1930. He had a distinguished career and was responsible for police arrangements when Royal visitors were the guests at Blythswood House. In 1928 Captain Robb was awarded the King's Police Medal.

THE ROBERTSON PARK, RENFREW.   A.3967.

64. *The Robertson Park.* This public park was the gift of the shipowner, Mr. William Robertson. The thirty-acre park was formally opened in October 1912. Mr. Robertson also provided a substantial iron railing around the grounds and placed gateways at the two main entrances. His two sons, Mr. John Robertson and Mr. Frank Robertson, added to their father's gift by presenting a flag, flagstaff and a large covered bandstand. At the opening ceremony the members of the Town Council and invited guests assembled in front of the Police Station in Inchinnan Road. Provost Robert Anderson presented Mr. Robertson with a golden key with which he opened the gate of the park. The Provost used a further golden key to open the gate of the bandstand. Before leaving the park, trees were planted by Mr. and Mrs. William Robertson. In addition Mrs. Robertson was presented with a silver spade to commemorate her husband's great benefaction to the people of Renfrew.

Park Gates, Renfrew.

65. *Park Gates, about 1920.* The gates shown here are those of the Paisley Road entrance to Robertson Park. These are the gates and railings which were provided by Mr. William Robertson when he presented the park to Renfrew. It was in 1909 that Mr. Robertson wrote to Provost Peter Ferguson and informed him that he had purchased a portion of ground at Longcroft and wished to present it to the people of Renfrew. Mr. Robertson also stated in his letter that he trusted the Town Council would accept and maintain it for all time as a public park for the burgh and that it would prove of value to the community.

Orchard Street, Renfrew.

66. *Orchard Street, 1917.* Children are shown here standing in the traffic-free street. It is likely that they would spend their 'Saturday penny' in the confectioner's shop on the right of the picture. At this time children had to make their own amusements as there were no television, videos or radios. They spent much time playing games – all of which had certain rules. However, these rules were often altered to suit circumstances. These games included hinch-cuddy-hinch (jumping on the backs of a row of bent bodies), hoppity-hop (hopping on one leg and trying to knock the opponent over), jinkers (played with a ball against a wall) and playing marbles. Orchard Street is so named because the land on which it was built was once part of the Royal Orchards in past centuries.

67. *Unveiling of the War Memorial.* Almost 20,000 people gathered at St. Andrew's Cross on the afternoon on 5th August 1922 to watch the unveiling of the burgh war memorial. Windows overlooking Hairst Street were filled with spectators and road traffic was temporarily halted. Shortly before 3 p.m. the procession comprising local ex-servicemen, members of the Memorial Committee, the Town Council and the Parish Council headed by the Burgh Band left the Council Chambers on their way to the Cross. The Reverend Robert Hill of the Free Church gave the dedication prayer, then the memorial was unveiled by Colonel Walter Brown. Silence fell as he pulled the cord and the flags which were draped round the memorial fell to the ground. Mr. Joseph Johnstone, Member of Parliament for East Renfrewshire, made a short speech after which the lament 'The Flowers of the Forest' was played by the pipers. After the Last Post had been sounded, members of the public came forward to lay wreaths and flowers at the base of the memorial.

HAIRST STREET AND WAR MEMORIAL, RENFREW.

68. *Hairst Street and War Memorial.* This shows a close-up of the war memorial on which are inscribed 169 names of those who were killed in the First World War 1914-1918. Following the lines of a Mercat Cross, the memorial is octagonal in shape, each of the sides forming sunk panels in which are incorporated the dedication panel and four panels with the names of the dead inscribed in leaded lettering. Two of the remaining panels have subjects half-life size carved in bas-relief, one symbolising 'Duty and Defence' and the other the 'Glorious Dead'. Over each diagonal corner of the 'chamber' are projected turrets on the face of which are carved the Royal Coat of Arms, Baron Renfrew's Arms, Blythswood Arms and Renfrew County Arms. The Scottish Lion Rampant with a shield bearing the Royal Burgh Coat of Arms can be seen at the top of the octagonal column of the memorial. The architect of the memorial was Mr. Hamilton Neil, F.R.I.B.A. and the contractors were Messrs. Scott and Rae, Glasgow. The sculptor was Mr. James Young of Glasgow.

69. *Provost Daniel Ferguson*. The man in the bowler hat who is seated in the open carriage on the left of this photograph was Daniel Ferguson, Provost of Renfrew from 1918 to 1924. He was also convener of Housing for eleven years, convener of Public Health for ten years and convener of Property and Improvements for seven years. In addition, he served as councillor for the Fourth Ward for 22 years. In December 1926 Ex-Provost Ferguson, who had retired from the Town Council in November of that year, was the guest of councillors and officials when he was publicly thanked for his years of faithful service to the town. Many notable events took place in Renfrew during Provost Ferguson's term of office. In 1919 'Homes for Heroes' cottage housing was commenced at Victory Gardens, the Victory Baths in Inchinnan Road were built in 1921 and the town was visited by H.R.H. The Duke of York (later King George VI) and H.R.H. The Princess Mary, daughter of King George V. In this photograph the carriage is passing in front of the Town Hall. The top-hatted coachman is looking at the photographer in a most suspicious manner! Seated beside him is Captain William Robb, the Chief Constable.

70. *Hairst Street.* A Paisley and District open-topped tramcar is shown here in this view of Hairst Street in 1924. The tramcar, number 23, is en route for Barrhead. Electric trams were first introduced between Glasgow and Renfrew in November 1902. An extension of this route to Porterfield Road was made in 1932. The trams ceased to operate in May 1957, and the rails were uplifted in 1962. The Paisley and District Company operated a local service between Renfrew Ferry and Speirsbridge. This was taken over by Glasgow in 1923. The only other form of transport to be seen here is the horse and cart on the opposite side of the street. The children, as always, are interested in what the photographer is doing.

BELL STREET, RENFREW.

71. *Bell Street.* This is a view of Bell Street in 1919. The stone cottages shown here were built in the 1860s. These cottages are still to be seen to-day while all of the tenements on the opposite side of the street have been demolished to make way for more modern buildings. However, the street is no longer illuminated by the gas lamp-posts. There is no traffic at all to be seen here and thus children were able to play in much greater safety than would be the case today.

72. *Demolition Scene*. Between 1926 and 1928 a considerable amount of work took place in High Street when widening took place and buildings were demolished. This photograph was taken in 1926. A report in the 'Paisley and Renfrewshire Gazette' of 30th June 1928 pointed out that with the demoliton of the former Co-operative Buildings in High Street, the appearance of this part of Renfrew had changed completely from what it had been a few months ago. In addition, the report mentioned that with the demoliton of Malloy's property the High Street from the Cross to Queen Street would be more than twice its former width. As a result of the improvements in High Street, the entrance to Renfrew was greatly improved and there was a reduction in the number of traffic jams which had frequently occurred. From April 1929 there was a double set of tramcar rails in High Street. Previously, there had only been a single line from High Street to Queen Street. It was now possible to have two trams stationed at the Cross instead of one having to wait at Queen Street.

73. *High Street and Cross, 1920s.* The spire of Renfrew Parish Church can be seen on the right. At this time it seems that people did not worry too much about the traffic, judging by the two men who are standing in the street. A solitary car is travelling down High Street towards the Cross.

74. *Staff of William Simons and Company, 1929.* This firm became famous as builders of hoppers and dredgers. It was among the first firms to invent a tool capable of deepening and smoothing the river bed and removing the debris. Those included in this photograph are R. Dick, J. McLure, J. Gray, J. Steven, J. Knight, J. Macgregor, J. Dunn, J.B. McGregor, R. Smart, A. Morton, D. Robertson, D. Macgregor, J. Campbell, J. Smith, R. Brown, J. McKenzie, D. Cree, H. Scott, H. Airlie, H. McMinagle, J. Russell, A. Paton, A. Bradley, A. Youill, R. Guthrie, P. McLachlan, D. McCracken, W. McIntyre, J. Youill, J. Findlay, J. Lyle and A. Crawford.

75. *Babcock and Wilcox Workers*. This shows workers leaving Babcock and Wilcox Ltd. in about 1930. This firm was founded in America by George Babcock and Stephen Wilcox in 1881. In 1882 the firm decided to establish works in the Glasgow area and soon made arrangements with the Singer Company at Clydebank whereby boiler plant could be produced there until suitable premises were found elsewhere. In 1891 the British Babcock and Wilcox Company was formed and their factory at Renfrew commenced production in 1897 when one thousand men were transferred from Singer's of Clydebank. One of the main attractions of the Renfrew site was the local market for marine boilers, cranes and similar products. There was also the added benefit of the ready supply of steel available in the west of Scotland. Babcock and Wilcox was not greatly affected by the trade depressions of the 1920s and the 1930s. As a result, the firm was able to expand and gained a world-wide reputation in the manufacture of a wide variety of engineering products.

76. *Renfrew Pipe Band.* Here is a photograph of the band in about 1930. It was founded in 1927 and at one time gained second place in the world competition for both piping and drumming events. The kilt worn by the members of the band is of the Clan McGregor tartan as a compliment to Mr. John McGregor, who was Provost of Renfrew when the band was founded. The bonnets are of black material with a green hackle. The hackles are the long feathers attached to the bonnets.